Printed in Great Britain
by Amazon

61530091R00071